LYRICAL POEMS OF LOVE

A collection of poems

by

Fanny Jasper Wallin

ISBN: 0-7596-7620-8

This book is printed on acid free paper.

1stBooks - rev. 01/07/02

DEDICATION

This book is dedicated to my loving parents, Robert (Bob) and Rose Jones Jasper, whom are both now deceased. Also, my deceased son, Thomas Frederick. Their genuine love and truth has been, and still is, a great source of inspiration in my life. I also want to thank both of my daughters, Regina, and Tomina, and my grandchildren, Brandon, Brandy, Rachel, and Caleb, for their encouragement, love and support. I also thank my husband, Tom, who has shown a great deal of patience, through both the good and bad years.

Last, but certainly not least, I want to give thanks, and express my appreciation to my Creator, Almighty God, who has given me the creative ability to write, sing, and create melodies.

CONTENTS

LOVE WON'T LET YOU FORGET WHO YOU ARE

Leanin' back, in his soft, easy chair,

He's finally made it, he's goin' somewhere;

But he knows, that he'd be, at the bottom of the line;

If not for her, her love, and her time.

Love won't let you, forget who you are,

Sometimes, it's easy, when you've made your mark;

But love will guide you, and shield you from harm;

Love won't let you, forget who you are.

He knows he'd be nothing', without her, by his side,

She follows behind him, as he rides the tide;

She gives him the strength, that he needs to be strong,

Without her love, he knows he couldn't go on.

Fanny Jasper Wallin

I'LL NEVER GET OVER YOU

I'll never get over you,
don't even ask me to,

Cause, the memories of you,
they're everywhere;

You're every breath I take,
you're every move I make;

You're the wind in my wings,
that carry me through.

In a world, full of hatred,
and a time full of strife;

You are my shelter,
you are my life;

Oh, I know, that you're gone,
but your spirit lives on;

For it guides me,
in everything I do.

When this life is over,
and I've been laid to rest;

You can say, that I've been happy,
you can say, that I've been blessed;

You have been my inspiration,
you have been my lock and key;

To a world, that's filled with love,
and integrity.

JOHN, IS THAT YOU

John, is that you?

Please tell me, it's true;

Where have you been for so long?

Have you come back to stay,
or were you passin' by this way?

John, please tell me, is that you?

You never left, as much as a notice,

When you left, you never even, said goodbye;

For many years, I have wondered, about you,

For many years, I've sat alone and cried.

I won't ask you to stay,

No, I won't stand in your way;

I know, someone is waitin' for you;

If I could just touch your face,

And watch the years all erase,

And take away, all the pain,
I put you through.

SOMEWHERE IN DENVER

Somewhere in Denver,
there's a man, living alone;

With no one to love him,
and no place, that he can call home;

Forgotten and troubled,
by a woman, who did him so wrong;

Somewhere in Denver,
there's a man, living alone.

I can see him in my mind,
as he comes home from work, all alone;

As he sits in a stare,
in his favorite chair, by the phone;

He remembers a time,
when the love of his life, was still home;

Somewhere in Denver,
there's a man, living alone.

He then picks up a paper,
which has laid by his side, for so long;

And the news, that it carried,
was news, that he couldn't dwell on;

So, he tears out her picture,
and he holds it in his arms, until dawn;

Somewhere in Denver,
there's a man, living alone.

NEVER BEFORE

The blue chair, you sat in,
the places you've been;

The sad in your eyes,
at the death of a friend;

A place at your table,
now empty and bare;

Oh, Lord, I'm wishin',
that you were still here.

Never before, have I missed anyone,
the way that I've missed you;

Never before, have I missed anyone,
the way that I've missed you;

Was it the kindness you showed,
to someone you saw in need?

Or the love of a child, without a home?

Or the stand, that you would take,
for the right, against the wrong?

Oh, Lord, I'm wishin', you were home.

When I go in your bedroom,
I can see you everywhere;

The same sheet, you lay on,
is still lying there;

The clothes, in your closet,
are strown everywhere;

Oh, Lord, I'm wishin',
that you were still here.

THE LORD WILL PROVIDE

I met an old lady,
on a journey one day;

She invited me in,
and asked me to stay;

There was food on her table,
and a warmth there inside;

I felt so at home,
that I wanted to cry.

I sensed she had little,
on which to rely;

And she knew, that I knew
by the look in her eyes;

She said, "Sit at my table,
and stay for awhile;

Enjoy my bounties,
the Lord will provide."

The Lord will provide,
the Lord will provide;

When you are in need,
Your needs he'll supply;

He'll never forsake you,
right down til' the end;

Cause, he knows where you're goin',
and he knows where you've been.

He knows when you're weak,
and he knows when you're worn;

He even remembers,
before you were born.

He'll stand beside you,
right down til' the end;

And you'll have the Lord,
forever a friend.

I'VE ONLY ONE ROSE

I saw an old man, with a rose in his hand,
as he knelt by a grave'stone one day;

His head was bowed low, and his eyes had lost their glow,
as he lay the rose on a grave.

I drew near to him, as the evening grew dim;

Cause, I wanted to hear, what he would say.

He said, "I've only one Rose,
and she was my life,

She was an angel, a sweet, caring wife;

But the Lord, up in heaven,
he loved her too;

So, I guess, this one rose,
will just have to do."

He said, "My Rose, wasn't greedy,
she'd give unto all;

She didn't want nothing,
want nothing at all;

She would give to a stranger,
the best that she had;

And if nothing were left,
she'd smile and be glad."

CAN I BORROW YOUR ARMS

Can I borrow your arms, to hold me tonight?

Would you loan me your lips, to kiss me goodnight?

I'll return them tomorrow, and make everything right,

If I can borrow your arms, to hold me tonight.

I've been looking a long time, for a sweet man like you,

With dark hair so curly, and bright eyes so blue;

You fit the description, yes, you seem so right,

Can I borrow your arms, to hold me tonight?

There are other men out there, so lonely and blue,

Reaching for someone, to give their love to;

They have arms, that could hold me, but it wouldn't be right,

Can I borrow your arms, to hold me tonight?

YOU'RE THE ONE THAT I SLEEP WITH— WHEN THE LIGHTS GO OUT AT NIGHT

There's just something about your memory,
that won't let me sleep at night,

Cause, I toss, and I turn,
at the flicker of a light;

I can't help, but think about you,
you made everything so right;

You're the one, that I sleep with,
when the lights go out at night.

When the lights go out at night,
you're the one that I see;

You're the one that keeps me warm,
as I drift off to sleep;

I remember, how you held me,
with your arms around me tight;

You're the one, that I sleep with,
when the lights go out at night.

I remember, how you held me,
with your arms around me tight;

And your touch, that was so tender,
that could light a fire so bright;

I can't help, but think about you,
you made everything so right;

You're the one, that I sleep with,
when the lights go out at night.

WHATEVER HAPPENED TO DALLAS

Sittin' on a wooden porch,
foundation almost gone;

Sat a sweet, old man,
who sang a sweet, old song;

He wasn't nothin' fancy,
as plain as he could be;

But let me tell you, here and now,
he meant the world to me.

He'd take the time to listen,
when you were down and out;

He'd tell you what was best for you,
there was never any doubt;

When you'd get down and lonely,
when you needed a friend;

You could count on Dallas,
until the very end.

Whatever happened to Dallas?

Did he go away?

Whatever happened to Dallas?

Will he be back someday?

Time can sometimes be fragile,
when you sit and let it stand still;

Somehow, you know that it's passing,
passing against your will;

Don’t count on another tomorrow,
to do what you can today;

It may be another tomorrow,
will slowly fade away.

I'VE BEEN WALKIN' THE ROAD OF HEARTACHE TOO LONG

I've been walkin' the road of heartache too long,
too long, way too long;

I've been singin' the song of sadness too strong,
too strong, way too strong.

I think it's time for me to travel on,

I've walked these lonely halls,
from dusk til' dawn;

Not really feelin' wanted or belonged;
I think it's time for me to travel on.

It's sad to be, where you don't want to be,

Knowin' full well, that you're not free;

Just tryin' to be the best, that you can be,

And holding fast to your integrity.

I'm leavin' all the best of me behind,

There's another hill, I'm tryin' hard to climb;

I'll not walk on another's shoes to find,

Not the way, that some have walked on mine.

MARIA, WON'T YOU PLEASE COME BACK HOME

His shirt had faded, from the sun beating down,
His face was weathered and dry;
His hands told a story, about a young man in time,
But I saw a tear in his eye.

His eyes looked toward heaven, in a soft, gentle stare,
As though, he were praying inside;
His lips, seem to quiver, as he murmured these words,
He said, "Maria, won't you please come back home?"

"Maria, won't you please come back home?
I just can't stand it anymore, with you gone;
I just can't live, without your love,
I've even told the Lord above;
Maria, won't you please come back home?"

"I can't forget our younger years,
And how you calmed, away my fears;
From all the trouble, that I'd get into;

You seemed to know, just what to do,
You could always see me through;

Maria, won't you please come back home?"

YOU'RE MY RAINBOW AFTER THE RAIN

You're my rainbow, after the rain,

You're my sunshine, after the pain;

You're the one, that made me live again,

You're my rainbow, after the rain.

Not so long ago, I was feelin' down and low,

With no where on earth, left to go;

But then you came along, and gave to me a song,

A song, that lingers on and on.

I don't think, that there ever could be,

Someone else, that special to me;

What you've done, you could never see,

Cause, you're light, shines only for me.

TRUE LOVE IS BETTER THAN GOLD

In your arms, there is strength of a mountain,

On your lips, there is wisdom untold;

In your eyes, there is glory forever,

Let me tell you, true love is better than gold.

In your smile, there's a sense of direction,

That can lead me to places unknown;

In your hands, lies a road map to guide me,

Let me tell you, true love is better than gold.

Better than gold, better than gold,

What on earth, could be better than gold?

If you'll look around to see,
I'm sure that you'll agree with me;

That true love is better than gold.

Sometimes, life can be a test,
when we find we're in a mess;

And some around you,
seem so bitter and cold;

If you'll look around to see,
I'm sure that you'll agree with me;

That true love is better than gold.

YOU HAVE TO DRAW FROM THE WELL

So, you don't need them anymore,
To you, they're just a daily chore,
Extra work, for you to have to do;
Yes, they're in their golden years,
But, they've shed a million tears,
All because, they cared so much for you.

So, you're grown, and on your own,
And you have that special home,
And a family, that's doing, oh, so well;
But, you can't give, and you can't take,
So, someday soon, your heart will break,
Cause, you didn't draw from the well.

Draw from the well of loving kindness,
Draw from the well of sweet success;
You didn't give back, what you were given,
In your years of true tenderness.
No, you didn't know, what you were doing,
But, someday, you will understand;
As sure, as there's a God, in the heavens,

Your life will deal back the same hand;

You have to draw, from the well of loving kindness,

You have to draw, from the well of sweet success;

You can't get back, what you've not given,

Throughout your years of tenderness.

VICTIM OF TIME

I met him, at the end of his driveway,

As he was picking up his daily mail;

His feet were dragging behind him,

And his body was looking so frail.

You could tell, he was doing some thinking,

Because, his mind seemed so far away;

I stopped for a moment, and watched him,

Cause, I didn't know the right words to say.

How could I say, "Good morning",
on such a bleak and dreary day?

How could I pretend a good feeling,
when I could see love slipping away?

He looked so alone and forsaken,

I could tell, he had a lot on his mind;

His dark hair, had all turned to silver,

And now, was a victim of time.

YOUR MEMORY IT FOLLOWS ME AROUND

Your memory, it follows me around,

It's everywhere I go, it's in the face,
that I don't know;

Your memory, it follows me around,

Every door, that I go through,
I always catch a glimpse of you;

Your memory, it follows me around.

We use to walk, side by side, close together,

I felt secure, in your arms, in stormy weather;

Though, you've gone away from me, I know,
you can still be found;

Cause, your memory, it follows me around.

It's in the things, that I have found,
It's in the sunset goin' down;

Your memory, it follows me around;

If I could choose, what I would do,

I'd spend my life, just lovin' you;

Cause, your memory, it follows me around.

BLUE EYES AND BLUE SKIES

Blue eyes, and blue skies,
are all that I see,

From a picture, so vivid,
in my memory;

Porch swings, and little things,
stand out in my mind,

And, so does a loved one,
with the passage of time.

The stars in the heavens,
they send down their light,

The moon shines a brightness,
to light up my night;

I love all the beauty,
that stands before me;

But, blue eyes, and blue skies,
are all that I see.

Blue eyes, and blue skies,
are all that I see,

Of a picture, I have,
of a sweet memory;

No, time can't erase,
what it took from me;

Cause, blue eyes, and blue skies,
are all that I see.

IT'S AMAZING WHAT TRUE LOVE CAN DO

Love can make a weak man strong,

It can keep you hangin' on,

When troubles have burdened you down;

It won't up, and walk away,

But stand by you, come what may;

It's amazing, what true love can do.

Some say love can be so cruel,

That it can take you for a fool,

But, I say, love is the best thing one could have;

It won't leave you in the end,

But will forever, be your friend;

It's amazing, what true love can do.

Love can make an old man cry,

It can make an eagle fly,

When the sun in the evenin' goes down;

It won't up, and walk away,

But stand by you, come what may;

It's amazing, what true love can do.

LET ME BE THE FIRST TO KNOW

You're giving all the signs, that you're leavin',

You're tryin', to not let it show;

But there's someone, that you're not revealin',

Cause, you're not sure, that you can let go.

Just be sure, that it's her, that you want dear,

Cause, when you leave, I'll no longer be found;

All you'll have, is just a lot of old memories',

Til' you die, and are hid in the ground.

Let me be the first to know,

Darlin', if you want to let go;

Don't scatter the shame,
and each other blame;

Just let me be the first to know.

We've shared good and bad, and everything we had,

We've walked over rough, rugged road;

If you feel, you can go on, and there you'll belong,

Then, let me be the first to know.

OH, BABY, HOW I LOVE JUST LOVIN' YOU

I hope, you're not too tired of me,

And my face, you long to see;

Cause, baby, I could never get tired of you.

You're forever on my mind,

You stay there all the time;

Oh, baby, how I love just lovin' you.

I love just lovin' you,

That's all I want to do;

Just bein' close, and bein' next to you.

I can't get too much of you,

How I love you, yes, I do;

Oh, baby, how I love just lovin' you.

I know, I'm quite a pest,

But, I'm not like some of the rest;

I'll not love you, then throw your love away.

If you're not content to stay,

Then, I'll soon be on my way;

Oh, baby, how I love just lovin' you.

THE DRIFTER

On the corner of Fifth and Vine,
a drifter wrote this rhyme;

He made a singer out of me.

I'll never forget the day,
this drifter use to say;

If you try hard,
the world will let you be.

This drifter was a man,
no one could understand;

But, he had lots of rhythm in his soul.

On the corner of Fifth and Vine,
a drifter wrote this rhyme;

He made a singer out of me.

Leanin' on a table,
in a crowded, old bar'room;

He beat out Kaliga,
while fumblin' with a broom;

The people there all loved him,
as they reached out their hand;

For they all knew this drifter,
was a special kind of man.

WANDERIN' HEART AND WANDERIN' EYES

Wanderin' heart and wanderin' eyes,
How you took me by surprise;
What you've done, you don't realize,
Wanderin' heart and wanderin' eyes.

I saw the look, and the desire,
I knew your heart, it was on fire;
The look you gave, you can't disguise,
Wanderin' heart and wanderin' eyes.

She was standing there, a beauty queen,
All blossomed out, like a flower in spring;
You didn't want, my heart to cry,
Wanderin' heart and wanderin' eyes.

I understand, you're just a man,
And you're part, of the maker's plan;
But my trust, in you has died,
Wanderin' heart and wanderin' eyes.

LOVE MADE HIM REMEMBER

Love made him remember,
to come back again;

He didn't ask no questions,
he just walked right in;

From where it all started,
here's where it ends;

Love made him remember,
to come back again.

I guess I'm the reason,
that he went away;

I gave him no reason,
for wanting to stay;

The Lord made something,
I don't want to end;

Love made him remember,
to come back again.

My door is always open,
to him at any time;

There'll be a key a'waitin',
for his hands to find;

The Lord, made something,
I don't want to end;

Love made him remember,
to come back again.

I JUST DON'T THINK

I love the feel, of your body,
next to mine dear;

I love the way, you hold me,
in your arms;

I love everything, that I see dear;

I love the way, you lead me,
with your charms.

I just don't think, that I could ever,
live without you;

I just don't think, that I'd know,
what to do;

But remember, the times,
we were together;

And the feelings, between me and you.

I love to walk, through the park,
hand in hand dear;

I love to watch, the sparkle,
in your eyes;

I love every, little, waking moment,

That you, are ever, by my side.

WE HAVE LOVE

We don't have a fancy home,
but we have love;

We don't have a fancy car,
but we have love;

What we have, make no mistake,

Is neither yours, nor ours to take;

What we have is pure, old-fashion love.

We have love, we have love,

Sent to us from God above;

With wings flyin' high,

Like the wings of a dove.

We have love, we have love,

Sent to us from God above;

What we have is pure, old-fashion love.

We don't have satin sheets,
to lie upon,

We don't worry, if what we say,
comes out all wrong;

What we have, make no mistake,

Is neither yours, nor ours to take;

What we have is pure, old-fashion love.

I WANNA' LOVE YOU AGAIN

I use to stand, in the doorway,
to wait for you, to get home;

You couldn't call,
but the clock on the wall,
was better, than having a phone.

We had our little way, of knowin',
how long, that we would be gone;

I'd work the fields,
and fix you hot meals,
but those days are over and gone.

I wanna' love you again,

Feel the same feelin' back then;

Thrill to the sound,
of your car pullin' in,

I wanna' love you again.

Time has changed, both of us dear,
but not the spark in your eye;

After fifteen years, I saw a tear,
and I knew you wanted to cry.

I had to hide my true feelins',
to make things easy for you;

But deep, down inside,
my heart knows I lied,

Cause, it felt the same way too.

THE DIFFERENCE BETWEEN TRUE LOVE AND A FRIEND

I wish I could tell you, that I love you,
I wish I could tell you, that I care;
But you see, I've found someone true dear,
Someone's life, that I want to share.

He came like the sun in the mornin',
To warm up the chill on my skin;
He came like a star in the evenin',
To light up my pathway again.

If there were two diamonds in a window,
One was rough, and the other one smooth;
Give me your honest opinion,
Just which one would you choose?

I loved you so much at one time dear,
I thought I'd never love again;
But, I didn't know the difference,
Between true love and a friend.

TWO BY TWO, NONE BY ONE, AND ONE BY THE ONE HE LOVED

He left me for her, and she left him for Tim,

But while they both were leavin',
there was Billy Joe and Jim;

Now Billy Joe and Jim, has another dad,

And life, for the two of them,
started pretty bad.

While the both of them were leavin',
another came along,

But it was with this one,
that he didn't stay too long;

So, then he met another,
that he wanted for his own;

Then came little Janie,
and baby John along.

I've mentioned two by two,
and now the none by one;

By now, I guess you're wonderin',
where is the other one?

Well, this is little Jeanie,
who has now turned twenty-one;

She's had no bed of roses,
but she's had her share of fun;

Tomorrow is her wedding,

and he's coming down today;

Yes, I forgot to tell you,

he's giving her away.

The moral of this story,
as you probably have guessed;

Is never let your life,
get in such a tangled mess;

You should follow rules and guidance,
from the good Lord, up above;

And you'll not see, no two by two's,
but only two in love.

TWENTY YEARS

He walked off, from the grave,

Twenty years of love, they'd saved;

Twenty years, of being close together,

But now, he must go home,
to be there all alone;

To face, the coming years,
of stormy weather.

Time means nothin' flat,
as he lies there on his back;

Starin' at her picture on the wall.

He thinks of years gone by,
as he begins to cry;

He says, "Oh, Lord, I need you,
when I call."

He knows, he must go on,
but all his strength is gone;

How can he stay alone,
and be without her,

But strength to him is given,
by the good Lord, up in heaven;

Now, he knows together,
means forever.

I, LOVE, AND YOU

What's wrong with the words,
I, love, and you?

Are you afraid to use them,
for fear you'll be untrue?

Are you afraid of what others think,
and things that they might tell?

If you are, then my dear friend,
you're locked within a cell.

I passed some people, on the street,
just the other day,

I smiled, and said, "I love you,"
in a warm, and friendly way;

They stood amazed, with mind half-dazed,
at what they thought they heard;

Did she say, "I love you,
are those the words we heard?"

Don't shy away from people,
from things you want to say;

For fear, that things you say,
they'll take the other way;

Tell your mother, that you love her,

Tell your daddy, that you care;

Tell your grandma, and your grandpa,

That they're in your every prayer.

Don't be afraid to say, "I love You,"

Though some, might not understand;

Cause, these three words, I, love, and you,

Are in the master's plan.

I CAN'T FORGET THIS MEMORY

There's someone in my memory,
that I just can't forget;

I often think about him,
he's in my memory yet;

He'd cuddle up against me,
and keep my body warm;

Every time I think of him,
a new love is born.

I can't forget this memory,
that's burnin' in my soul;

Just to have him back again,
I'd trade all wealth or gold;

The better things in life are free,
but, oh, what he meant to me;

I can't forget this memory,
that's burnin' in my soul.

The bed we shared together,
has turned from warm to cold;

The place where he lay his head,
he lays his head no more;

There was a little window,
that he use to love;

But, there exists no window now,
only from above.

THERE'S NOTHING IMPOSSIBLE WITH YOU

There's nothing impossible with you,
You're a dream among dreams come true;
You're everything asked for and more;
There's nothing impossible with you.

I've dreamed all my life many dreams,
But you're a dream among dreams it seems;
You give all your best and more too;
There's nothing impossible with you.

When this life is over for me,
The best is still yet to be;
To know you has made my life true;
There's nothing impossible with you.

THERE IS NO ONE-NO ONE LIKE YOU

There is no one, no one like you,

You're a fairy tale, a dream come true;

Why, you always know what to do,

There is no one, no one like you.

I've known a few loves in my time,

Their love was good, but not mine;

But, when I found you, someone so true,

I knew that I'd always love you.

The angels in heaven were surely watchin',

When your mother gave birth to you;

Cause, there's no one on earth,
could do what you do,

And love me, the way I love you.

I CAN'T IMAGINE YOU LOVIN' ME

I imagine leaves in the wind,

I imagine places, that I've been;

I imagine everything I see,

But, I can't imagine you lovin' me.

I can't imagine you lovin' me,

It's more than anyone can see;

Sometimes, I close my eyes,
to picture what I see;

Cause, I can't imagine you lovin' me.

You're just like a fairy tale come true,

You prove yourself in all you say and do;

I've wondered in my mind, how this could be,

Cause, I can't imagine you lovin' me.

IT'S SAD TO SEE A MAN LEFT ALONE

As I was goin' down a country road,

I saw a man with a heavy load;

His eyes were starin' out, at fields of green,

It was the humblest sight, I'd ever seen.

I thought I'd stop, and talk awhile,

Cause, to talk, was just my style;

He said, "Do you see what I see?"

This land was meant for her and me.

It's sad to see a man left alone,
alone, all alone;

It's sad to see a man left alone,
alone, all alone.

He said, "I'm glad you stopped today,

It helped to pass the time away;

There's somethin' in your smile,
that I can see;

It helps me hold her memory."

He said, "You know,
I was feelin' bad today,

Until you came, and passed my way;

But now, I feel I can go on,

It seems as though, it were a song."

HIGH TIME FOR LOVE

In the Bible, it says,
there's a time for everything,

Flowers to bloom, robins to sing;

Raindrops to fall,
from heaven up above;

I think that it's high time for love.

Have you walked someone old,
or a child, a story told?

Said, "I love you," in a meaningful way;

Did you give of yourself,
to help somebody else?

I think that it's high time for love.

While you're sittin' there feelin',
sorry for yourself,

Somebody out there,
Is needin' your help;

It may be someone,
who has lost everything;

What little, you could give,
you stand so much to gain.

The Lord, watches people,
from every walk of life;

Those who are loving,
and those full of strife;

If you know, that he's watchin',
from heaven up above;

You'll know, that it's high time for love.

SOMEBODY SAD

Have you ever been around somebody sad?
It can make you count the blessings you once had;
If you would stop to see, and not ignore his misery;
You would find it wasn't all that bad.

The Lord has a way to help us all;
He stands by to catch us when we fall;
We never get too big, or ever stand too tall;
Yes, the Lord has a way to help us all.

Susie's been gone, one year yesterday;
Grandpa just retired, and received his check today;
Mama's in the kitchen, thinking of her lonesome past;
Bobby's in the bedroom, his body in a cast.

Lord, how we need you, you're our dearest friend;
Lord, will you help us all, until the final end?
There's no one on earth, to whom an earthling man can turn;
Make us see the need to pray, and blessings rightfully earn.

I DON'T MIND THE RUNNY NOSE

A little boy, once came to me,
He said, "Teacher, you're okay;
But I've been here, almost one year,
And I've never heard you say."
I said, "Say what, my little boy?"
He said, "I thought you knew;
If I were just a bigger boy,
You'd say you loved me too."

His little nose was runny,
His hair was all a mess;
His clothes were torn and shattered,
But covered with a vest;
I put my arms around him,
Thoughts runnin' through my mind;
Someday, he'd be a handsome man,
Some girl would seek to find.

No, I don't mind the runny nose,
And I don't mind the grit;
And I don't mind the lovin',

From any child I get;

To me, he's somethin' special,

A love that's hard to find;

And when you need to talk to him,

He'll always find the time.

He put his little hand in mine,

He said, "Teacher, you are oh, so kind;

But there's one thing, that I must confess,

I put you to the test;

No, you don't have to say you care,

I see it here, and everywhere;

I see it in the things you do,

Dear Teacher, I love you."

OLD-FASHIONED GENTLEMAN

There was a man, with heart of gold,

When, but a child, I knew;

Strong and rough, but gentle touch,

To all, who were in view.

He sang and played sweet music,

And sat me on his knee;

To tell me of a story,

When he was only three.

He sadly spoke of mother,

And how his heart was broke;

To live a life of sixty years,

Not having heard her spoke.

He was an old-fashioned gentleman,

Little children all had learned;

With overalls, and railroad hat;

And love for which they yearned.

Now the story has all ended,

And he's been laid to rest;

But whatever comes along in life,

His deeds will manifest.

ABOUT THE AUTHOR

Fanny Jasper Wallin studied language, poetry, and other fine arts at Richmond Kentucky University, where she came under the influence of some of the greatest, and most qualified Professors of the English Language. For over thirty years, she worked as an Elementary Teacher, having specialized in Special Education, and Rehabilitation. During this same period of time, she became interested in music and recording, and has written many lyrical poems, of which many have been previously set to music. She continues to write lyrical poems to this day.

www.ingramcontent.com/pod-product-compliance
Ingram Content Group UK Ltd.
Pitfield, Milton Keynes, MK11 3LW, UK
UKHW041934190726
13854UKWH00004B/1578

9 780759 676206